Navigating the Internet Jungle

Proceed with Caution

Part One
Starting an Online Business

By Nancy N. Wilson

Publisher's Notes

Navigating the Internet Jungle
Proceed with Caution
Part One – Starting an Online Business

By Nancy N. Wilson

Cover by pixelstudio

© Blurtigo Holdings, LLC
4th Edition – April 2016

ISBN-13: 978-1532839214

Originally published until the title of
Starting an Online Business

Published in United States of America

Disclaimer and Terms of Use:
The Author and Publisher have strived to be as accurate and complete as possible in the creation of this book. While all attempts have been made to verify information provided in this publication, the Author and Publisher assume no responsibility for errors, omissions, or contrary interpretation of the subject matter herein. Perceived slights of specific persons, peoples, or organizations are unintentional.

This material is designed to provide general information about the subject matter covered. The author and publisher are not engaged in rendering legal, financial, medical, or psychological advice. If expert assistance is required in these areas, the services of a professional should be sought.

IMAGES

Thank You – © ArenaCreative – StockFresh

I'm Going to Make You Rich – © iqoncept – BigStock.com

Hacker - © aetb – BigStock.com

… for buying my book.
If you enjoy it, please take a minute
and post a review on the platform where
you made your purchase

Navigating the Internet Jungle

For a complete list of my published books,
please, visit my website
http://www.nancynwilson.com

Nancy N. Wilson

LIKE My Page on Facebook
https://www.facebook.com/NancyNWilsonAuthor/

DEDICATION

To everyone who wants to start an Online business!

My hope is that this book will help you get through the early stage in the shortest time possible, without being caught by the predators who are constantly on the lookout for new players, and that it will help you avoid some of the pitfalls that I experienced in my personal journey of *Navigating the Internet Jungle.*

All the Best – Stay Safe!

TABLE OF CONTENTS

INTRODUCTION

Working from home has become the new "American Dream." After all, over a decade has passed since the "turn of the Century" and things are decidedly different now. Going into the office every day and continually doing what others require you to do, no longer have the appeal they once had.

You want to get up every morning, make a fresh pot of coffee, put on comfortable clothes (or stay in your PJs), and start making money working from your personal computer. All you need is the right opportunity – right? Well . . . maybe . . . maybe not.

This book was written to get you "up close and personal" with that dream and to help you decide whether, or not, it is a path you actually want to take.

This dream is unquestionably the siren's song of the 21st Century. Everyday hundreds, thousands, maybe hundreds of thousands of people decide to explore the idea of working from home (virtual employment) or starting their own home-based business online.

It is certainly doable. Many people with the same dream have ventured forth into this new territory. Some of those adventuresome souls have been marginally successful – others wildly successful.

Some came from the tech world and hit the ground running because they already knew how to build Websites and how to navigate the Internet with ease. Or, at the very least, they knew the in's and out's of operating a computer.

There were others for whom this was totally uncharted territory. They were forced to climb a seriously steep learning curve; but, they were willing to do whatever was necessary.

They believed the opportunities were there for the taking; they had a brilliant idea for an Internet business; and/or their entrepreneurial spirit was so strong that they were sure they could find a way to follow their dream.

It does not matter which group best describes you. To be honest, the Internet is the great equalizer. Whether a person succeeds or fails in his/her endeavor does not seem to be closely connected to any level of formal education. The big success stories and abysmal failures belong to high school dropouts and people with advanced college degrees, plus everything in-between.

Characteristics Shared by the Successful

There are specific characteristics shared by those who have been successful on the Internet.

How many of the characteristics do you have?

- They are self-starters. They understand that they have to get up, go to work, and stay at work every day (at least five days a week – usually more).
- They are optimistic by nature and maintain a positive outlook regardless of what happens.
- They love to tackle new things and enjoy the challenge of a steep learning curve.
- They study the business environmental threats and prepare themselves to face the dangers that may arise.
- They understand the financial risks and are willing and able to deal with the ebb and flow of their revenue stream, which is part of any entrepreneurial venture.
- They never give up and have the ability to stay the course when faced with new challenges and obstacles day-after-day.

If you have already ventured into the "Internet Jungle" on an exploratory mission, or have actually taken steps to start your Internet business – you have demonstrated that you are an optimistic self-starter. Without an optimistic approach to life, you would never have considered the possibility of following this dream in the first place.

Obviously you are willing to learn because you are seeking information through articles and books like this one. In other words, you have already demonstrated some of the necessary characteristics required to be successful; nevertheless, you must be prepared for the challenges ahead because it is not an easy road.

Establishing an Internet business is the equivalent of entering a wild jungle – a wild electronic jungle. Survival and success in this jungle will be dependent on your ability to recognize the dangers and to develop the necessary survival skills to combat those dangers.

If you are ready to take this on. . .
Let's begin the journey.

PART ONE

PROCEED WITH CAUTION

In all likelihood, you will encounter the greatest dangers early on when you are most vulnerable. Because of your lack of experience and your intense desire to succeed, you will be eager to find someone to show you the way; and, therein lay the danger.

Dangers Are Everywhere

Let me start with the story about an extremely dangerous predator that almost ate me alive within the first 48 hours of my initial foray into the Internet Jungle. I was prime, delicious game for the taking.

In early 2012, I was supporting my disabled son and his three-year-old daughter, when I lost my job without warning. It was devastating because even though I have many years of experience and an MBA from Thunderbird School of Global Management, I was years beyond the desirable age for any company to consider hiring me.

Finding some way to earn a living was imperative and there was absolutely nothing on the horizon. It was a difficult time filled with uncertainty, worry, and a terrible feeling of defeat.

For several months, my e-mail had been filled with promises of easy riches through the Internet. I had noticed them in the evenings when I checked my e-mail and quickly deleted them; but, now I was desperate. I decided that maybe I should consider all possibilities. I told myself that I was well-educated, had serious business savvy, and lots of experience – surely there would be something that would work for me.

I found a company that looked promising. The link was: www.indigitalworks.com. Frankly, I can't remember what they promised, I only know that it sounded like something I could do and would allow me to create a steady income.

I paid the $97.00 and with eager anticipation clicked into the site. Almost immediately there was a pop-up box that offered a free coaching session to get me started, which sounded like a good idea since I had no clue about how to proceed.

That FREE coaching session turned out to be the trap that snagged me so the predator could devour me financially - one giant bite at a time.

The predator was a "coaching company" that promised to guide me through the process of setting up an online business that would produce a sizeable income in six months or less. I knew I needed help to generate the income I desperately needed. They captured my interest, sweet talked me into the program by saying things like I was just the type of person they were looking for, and locked me in for $7,500 – even though my instincts were screaming – BE CAREFUL!

I am sure you are saying to yourself, "How could this woman have been so incredibly stupid?" I have asked myself that a thousand times. My only excuse is that I was blinded by my desperation, which made me extremely vulnerable . . . and they were good! Their system for capturing their prey was well-honed and hard to resist even for an intelligent, well-educated woman like me (and many others).

This is a long story that I will truncate and conclude by saying that by my fourth day into the lair, I realized I had made a horrible mistake. When I asked for my money back, I was told "no" because the three day grace period had expired.

I was furious with them for duping me and more furious with myself for being duped! I decided that I was not going to lose my money and started a relentless campaign to get it back. Luckily I finally won the battle; but, it took a lot of time, energy, and many sleepless nights over a six-week period. Frankly, I was lucky!

I wish I could say that was the only mistake I made and the only money I spent foolishly, but it wasn't. Over the next 12 months, I spent almost $7,000 on books, training, and software packages as I looked for the magic bullet that would help me make the fortune that was being promised over and over again.

Guess what, I never found the magic bullet. But, what I learned was incredibly valuable. I have compiled many of the lessons in this book. Hopefully they will be useful to you and prevent you from making some of the same mistakes.

When trekking through the Internet Jungle . . .

always proceed with caution!

In order to help you do that, the book describes the different types of predators you may face; the traps that have been baited and set; and the hidden dangers that await you. The only way to survive them relatively unscathed is to have the ability to recognize them instantly and avoid being caught and devoured.

Each chapter covers a specific type of danger.

- Predators on the Prowl
- Ferocious Bears and Sneaky Snakes
- Natives – Friendly and Not-so-Friendly
- The Cannibals
- Legitimate Internet Gurus
- Shiny Objects

Enter the journey with an open mind, a determined spirit, and the excitement that can only be experienced when beginning the adventure of a lifetime.

Good luck!

Chapter 1
Work-at-Home Jobs

Danger – Predators on the Prowl

Many newbies who are searching the Internet for opportunities are not looking for a full-fledged business opportunity. They are looking for a way to stay at home with their young children; supplement their spouse's income; help put a child through college; or find a way to retire comfortably and still make a contribution.

The members of this group are prime targets for the shady characters that are lay in wait with offers of enticing job opportunities for the unwary. They understand the group's vulnerability and they start to salivate as they think about the innocent prey that will soon be in their clutches.

There are legitimate "work-at-home" jobs available in a wide variety of industries, for all preferences, and all skill levels; but, many of the "opportunities" are scams! There are almost 60 fraudulent jobs to every one legitimate job.

The challenge is to figure out which ones are legitimate, and which ones are simply scams that trick you into believing you will receive one thing; and provide you with something entirely different (or nothing) while the perpetrator walks away with your money.

The real jobs that pay well are few and far between. If you have decided this is something that you genuinely want to do, do not give up. There are legitimate jobs that you would enjoy and that pay well; but, there is a chance you will have to create the "perfect fit" job yourself.

High Danger Alert: When considering an opportunity, any of the following should raise a big red flag – delete immediately!

- The requirement to send money for materials.
- The company is unwilling to answer your questions.
- The offer (or promise) of an exceptionally high salary in return for no skills, no experience, and minimal responsibilities or job requirements.
- If sounds too good to be true.

Being forewarned is forearmed. The following examples are typical of advertisements that can catch you off guard and allow these predators to happily take your money.

Online Job Scams

Craft or Assembly Jobs

This predator appeals to talented, creative people and those who are skilled at using hand tools. If you happen to fall into that group, the promise of a solid income for doing what you already know how to do is extremely attractive – in fact, almost irresistible. It feels like the perfect opportunity.

WAIT! There are some things that you don't know, but you need to know before you take another step!

The headline promises free materials to be used in the production of a product that will be sent to the employer – for which you will be paid. BUT – you must read the fine print carefully.

There is always a required investment for equipment or supplies. The investment can be anything from a few dollars to a few hundred dollars. This is what they are actually selling – and there is always a "no return policy" for the equipment and supplies.

And . . . that is not all. There is more than one way for this shady character to get you.

At the very bottom, in even tinier print well below the scroll line, there will be a statement that reads something like: "All work must meet quality standards." And, that is the trap! Your work will never meet their quality standards.

You buy the equipment or supplies, you put your heart and soul into creating the products exactly as directed, and you never see a single dollar for the products that you send.

The even bigger trap is that you have no legal recourse. When you agreed to purchase the equipment or supplies, the "no return policy" was clearly spelled out. You also agreed to meet the "quality standards" that were required. They are in the clear legally. There is nothing you can do.

Unfortunately, this scam is clouding a legitimate business avenue. There is a large market for hand-crafted products. Many people are earning a respectable living creating and marketing those products. The possibilities are endless.

So, if you have the talent to make quality hand-crafted products and the ability to market them – start and run your own business. Do not get caught up in this scam. You will never make money using your talents to assemble products for these tigers.

Medical Billing

Another catchy headline that draws in a lot of unsuspecting newbies is: "Job explosion in the Health Care Industry!!!!!!!" Note the exclamation points, which are always there. You will see these advertisements in newspapers, magazines and, of course, on the Internet.

Everyone is concerned about soaring medical costs, and this advertisement captures attention by promising to pay exceptionally well for jobs that will help lower the cost of health care. You need a job . . . and the health care world needs you. WOW! What could be better than that?

They explain that the overwhelming amount of required paperwork in the health care industry is the cause of inflated health care costs. A new and innovative technology that allows electronic claim processing will help solve this problem.

If you fall for this, you will pay the price. There is no truth what-so-ever in their statement. The medical profession already has electronic billing in place, and it is handled by a few well-established companies across the U.S. It is a subscription service for doctors that has been available since the late 1980's.

You will be required to make an investment of $1,000 to $10,000 for this golden opportunity; but, they promise it is worth it because, "You will be able to work part-time, at your own pace, and make tons of money." Does that sound realistic? In what world would that be possible? Business simply does not work like that – not even on the Internet.

If you take the bait, you will receive a brochure, an application, some discs, a contract, disclosure statements, basic instructions on how to set up the business, and testimonial letters from those who have succeeded beyond anything they thought was possible (all bogus).

What you will not have are clients! That will be up to you. Imagine trying to compete with large companies who have been in the medical billing business for years.

Data Entry

If you are proficient with numbers and have strong computer skills, this can be particularly appealing. Imagine spending a few hours a day in the comfort of your home putting numbers in columns and making enough money to pay those pesky monthly bills. Unfortunately....that is not likely to happen.

This is not to say that there are NO data entry jobs available. However, you will not be signing up for one of them by answering the slick ads that promise you a data entry job by signing up for one of their courses. These courses have absolutely nothing to do with data entry.

If you believe this shady character and pay for the course, you will receive the course either electronically or on CD's or DVD's. Then, SURPRISE – the course will teach you how to find and sign up for affiliate programs. (BTW – that information is readily available on the Internet for FREE).

As part of the course, you will be instructed how to set up advertisements in Google Ad Words. (Beware – there are free instructions for this on the Internet).

They will lead you to believe that ads on Google will cost $.01 each, but the ads are essentially useless. The ads may cost one penny per click; but, they will be listed on page 15 where they are unlikely to be seen. If, by any stroke of luck, they are clicked on, I guarantee the cost will be more than one penny.

The bottom line is that if you buy, you will pay for a course that will not be what is promised.

Affiliate marketing is legitimate and can be an extremely lucrative Internet business; but, it is difficult to set up and takes time to generate a decent income. What these shady characters fail to mention in their courses is that to launch and establish a successful affiliate marketing business requires a minimum of one hundred+ hours each week over an extended period of time.

Writers Wanted

This fierce and talented predator is adept at trapping his prey because there is an endless supply of people who want to write and be published.

The information age has created a never-ending need for people who can write quality articles, books, and reports on a variety of subjects. But, these advertisements are not really looking for writers. They are looking for vulnerable, naive "wannabe" writers who want to get their "work" published any way they can.

They are usually selling one of two things:

- A writing course of some kind.
- A list of places to sell your writing.

If you think you have talent and seriously want to write, hone your skills by taking courses at the local community college or seek out a writer who is giving private lessons, and practice – practice – practice. The more you write, the better you will be. All successful writers have paid their dues, and you must do the same.

You will not get a writing job by taking a course from this kind of solicitation or buying a list of places to submit your writing.

There are legitimate writing jobs – such as writing blog posts and reviews.

Check out the following:

- https://payperpost.com/

Gain as much experience as you can, all the while refining your skills.

You may also want to check out some legitimate freelance writing websites such as

- https://outsource.com/
- www.freelancewriting.com
- www.writersweekly.com
- www.ezinearticles.com.

Online Searches

"Work from home. Be your own boss and earn $500 to $1,000 a week or more running Internet searches and completing forms. What do you have to lose? You can start today for only a small shipping and handling fee."

It is no surprise that this ad draws a lot of attention.

The reality is that you have a lot to lose. The company has no connection to any well-known search engine (Google, Bing, Yahoo, Safari, etc.) The goal is to get your credit card information by getting you to pay the small shipping and handling fee. Once they have your information they can use it to charge recurring fees on your credit card and who knows what else!

Secret Shopper (Mystery Shopper)

The scam is one that can be found everywhere in the Internet Jungle. I am fairly sure that I get at least one of these a week, maybe more. It has broad appeal, and when you are a newbie in the jungle, it sounds like a good idea. Especially since being a "secret shopper" is a legitimate job – and who doesn't like to shop?

The idea of shopping with other people's money and getting PAID to do it is a huge temptation. The promise of making large sums of money for only a few hours of work (shopping) each week is tough to ignore. Plus, with no experience necessary and no educational requirements, you can see why it appeals to a broad spectrum of people.

One tell-tale sign of a job scam is the requirement to purchase training supplies or a training course before you start the job. Legitimate secret shopper companies will NEVER require such purchases. However, some of the scams do not require the purchase of training materials either, so be extra careful!

See the advice below from the Federal Trade Commission (FTC) for anyone interested in being a secret shopper:

The truth is that it is unnecessary to pay money to anyone to get into the mystery shopper business. The shopping certification offered in advertising or unsolicited email is almost always worthless. A list of companies that hire mystery shoppers is available for free; and legitimate mystery shopper jobs are on the Internet for free. Consumers who try to get a refund from promoters of mystery shopping jobs usually are out of luck. Either the business doesn't return the phone calls, or if it does, it is to try another pitch.

Rebate Processor

This is sold as a full-time online job from home that allows you to process rebates all day, every day from the comfort of your home that will generate hundreds of dollars an hour once you learn the system. No experience or particular skills required – and you can work as much or as little as your choose. All you have to do is pay the $97 (or more) sign-up fee.

They take your money, and you get nothing in return – a total scam.

Online Surveys

Earn $150 a day! Earn $750 a week! In the comfort of your home, sip coffee and fill out surveys.

Sounds too good to be true. Right? That is because it is!

There are companies that are willing to pay for market research through online surveys, but don't fall for this scam. You will be disappointed. **Do not fall for the hype!**

They promise you quick money for very little work. The ploy is that by spending a few minutes each day, you will develop an excellent income stream. How nice, that would be! The reality is that online surveys are often quite long, and take time to complete.

All you have to do is pay $24.95 to learn how to do this. For 100 people who buy, they make $2,495. Their goal is to get thousands of people to pay for their worthless information.

There are legitimate online survey companies, but finding them is almost impossible. If you type "online surveys" into Google search, you will get 16,800,000 results and there is no way of screening out the legitimate ones.

Even with a high ranking on a ranking site does not make them legitimate. Ranking sites may be middlemen who are paid commissions for referrals – so the ranking is not necessarily valid or reliable.

Work At Home E-mail Solicitations

There is another common type of "job offering" that you may receive. It simply appears (unsolicited) in your email inbox and looks fairly harmless (see sample below that I received earlier this year):

> joslyn3662@terra.com
> 6:30 PM (1 hour ago)
>
> Hello Wilson,
> Thousands of people across the nation are seeking work at home positions in the new year. Some programs require up-front costs yet others don't cost anything to start. You can start this position today without having to pay one penny.
>
> Start the new year off right and apply for this position without having to pay any start-up fees or overhead. The only catch is there is a limited amount of positions available so fill out the application and claim your placement before all spots are taken.
>
> http://topinfojobs.info
>
> To Your Success,
> joslyn thompson
> Work at Home Tips

No upfront investment required; no request for personal information; the email address looks authentic – but is it worth taking the risk. I didn't think so, but thought I would check it out anyway.

I tested it by pasting the web address into Google's search bar and found a notice from GoDaddy that the domain name was available (up for auction) – as of 6/21/2013. I also checked the email address (invalid); the name, Joslyn Thompson; and the tag line "Work at Home Tips." None of them had anything to do with job placement.

My instincts were correct; but, I was tempted. The sense of urgency (limited amount of positions) suckered me in.

"Paid-to-Use" Employment Programs and Memberships

If you have been at the online job search for a while with no success at finding a suitable fit and possibly having been scammed once or twice, you may be tempted to turn to websites that offer *"instant employment, prescreened job offers, with guaranteed success to all applicants."*

These programs make it seem extremely easy (too easy). There are no application forms, no interviews, and no real evaluation of your skills. Sounds suspicious? – Well, it is. All they want is for you to pay the "one-time membership fee" for their services.

You receive a welcome letter with your user name and password. You breathe a sigh of relief believing that you will finally find work and once again be able to pay your bills. Unfortunately, most of these job databases are scams. As you get into the job search process on these Websites, you will probably find some or all of the following:

They may have job listings, but applying for them and actually getting a job is not as easy as they make it seem in their sales pitch.

- The job postings are rarely updated.
- The jobs are not well-screened.
- There is often an investment required.
- Accurate job descriptions are usually not included.

In many cases, you could have found the same listings on a free resource site – which is probably where they found them.

If you want to use a job bank database, use the free ones. Below are some that you can try (but be careful even with these).

- www.careerbuilders.com
- www.Monster.com
- www.guru.com
- www.eLance.com

Career Builders, one of the larger, well-known companies listed above, includes the following disclaimer on jobs they consider "non-traditional."

NON-TRADITIONAL JOB - This opportunity is not a traditional job opportunity. There may be a required fee or investment of money and time to generate income. It may be a service, education, counseling, or simply information. CareerBuilder is committed to allowing only legitimate opportunities on our site, but we encourage you to investigate each opportunity thoroughly before committing money or time or releasing sensitive personal information. Ultimately, you are responsible for your decisions. Please alert us to any opportunities you have questions about by using the "Report This Job" link present on each job posting.

In other words, move forward at your own risk. You cannot go after Career Builders if you get caught in a scam.

Protect Yourself from Work-at-Home Job Scams

As clearly shown in the previous section, the predators lurking in the Internet bushes are waiting to take advantage of anyone who does not recognize them for what they are. The traps are baited and set with the promise of plentiful work-at-home job opportunities.

There are some decent work-at-home jobs available; but, the challenge is to find the legitimate job offers that also fit well with your interests, skills, and goals,

Use the following steps to test for legitimacy:

1. Check the E-mail Address

The most effective work-at-home scams will try to appear legitimate by using what appears to be a real company web address. If it is legitimate, you should see the company's name as the domain name. If it is an individual's name or if the company name has extended characters – delete immediately.

Even if it has a company domain name; but, something seems off, don't do anything until you at least type the company name into Google and see what pops up.

NEVER, NEVER send your personal information or resume to a Hotmail or Gmail address. Those are free accounts that anyone can open. If they are a legitimate company, they will have a "company.com" address.

2. Apply the Q & A Test

If you find a company that seems like a solid potential employer, give them the Q & A Test.

You are probably good to go, if they can answer the following questions to your satisfaction:

→ **Where is the company located?** This is essential since you will be connected with your employer electronically rather than physically.

→ **Does the company have a Website?** This is critical. You should start with the Website to get a clear understanding of what the company does. It is a check on their credibility.

→ **Is there a cost involved?** Legitimate jobs do not typically require an investment. They should pay you for your time, talent, and experience.

→ **What is the job description?** What is required in order to get paid? Legitimate jobs have a job description of some kind. What are the tasks you will be expected to perform? If they can't give you a reasonable description in a few sentences and a detailed list of required tasks, walk away.

→ **Will there be training to get you started?** Is the training paid or unpaid? The answer to this question will vary depending on the responsibilities involved. (With legitimate jobs, there is usually some kind of training period and often it is unpaid – so don't let this throw you.)

→ **Who will be my supervisor (report to)?** Many times there will be more than one partner in an online business. You need to know who will supply you with instructions and directions.

→ **How will I receive instructions?** You may receive instructions by email or by way of an instant messaging service.

→ **Is the position salaried, commission, or hourly?** For commission – what is the percentage and are there quotas? For hourly – how are the hours tracked and reported?

→ **How will you be paid and the payment schedule?** Will you be paid by check or direct deposit? What is the payment schedule? Every legitimate company or individual employer has regular and specified pay periods – every week, every two weeks, on the 1st and 15th, or every month. (Any one of those pay period options is legitimate.)

→ **When will I get my first paycheck?** Be sure to get clarity on this question.

3. Check for Complaints and Negative Press

It is critical that you check the Internet for complaints or negative "press" the company may have received – including any reported scams.

You should check the following websites for reported scams: http://www.scambook.com/search and http://www.scambusters.org.

Read what others on the Internet have to say about the company (or person). For example, place the company's name with the word *complaints* in Google's search bar – see what comes up.

You will also want to check out the company with the local consumer protection agency, the State Attorney General, and the Better Business Bureau: www.bbb.org/ - not only in the state where the company is located, but also where you live.

Your search can tell you whether complaints have been filed; but, just because no complaints show up is no guarantee that the company is legitimate. Unscrupulous companies settle complaints out of court, change their names, and move to avoid detection.

4. Trust Your Instincts

Finally, pay attention to your instincts, if you are uneasy for any reason, or you know you need to be careful, walk away!

Websites and/or forums can help in your search for legitimate businesses. Always use reputable resources in your search.

Below is a list that you can use to begin your search.

- http://www.dress4Success.com/
- http://www.wahm.com/forum/

Please NOTE: The above sites have been included for informational purposes only. Be wise in your use of them and in your acceptance of anything that you read. We do not guarantee their reputations or recommendations – be careful and do your homework before accepting any offers.

CHAPTER 2

FINDING A LEGITIMATE BUSINESS OPPORTUNITY

Danger - Ferocious Bears

There are two primary situations that can make people particularly vulnerable to the ferocious bears that are offering business opportunities on the Internet.

- **An individual has become unemployed** – often without warning. S/he desperately needs a job that will generate a nice income stream to support herself (himself) and in many cases a family, as well.

- **An individual is tired of working for others (the corporate slave) and wants to be the boss.** The person wants to give the orders, not take them; and, to make decisions, not carry out the decisions of others. The decision has been made – it is time to be the captain of the ship and master of his/her own destiny.

Both of those situations can be powerful drivers for people to begin the search for Internet business opportunities.

If you identify with one of those situations, you are probably not only ambitious, but also willing to roll up your sleeves and do whatever it takes to make an Internet business thrive.

Ambition, regardless of the motivator, is a primary factor in why people succeed, but it can be dangerous if it drives you to throw caution to the wind and make rash decisions that will literally come back to bite you. An eagerness to work at home and to be successful can cause you to forget that you are venturing into a jungle that is fraught with danger.

There are big ugly bears out there just waiting for you to get careless – hoping that you think starting an Internet business is going to be easy and that it will also bring in tons of money quickly.

All they need is for you to forget for one minute that they are out to get you. They are waiting for you to let ambition and/or desperation cloud your judgment and cause you to fall into the trap of making unwise, un-informed decisions.

For every ambitious, hard-working, honest, Internet entrepreneur out there, there are at least a hundred under-handed, ferocious bears waiting to take advantage of them.

The bears that live and, unfortunately, thrive in the Internet Jungle come in many varieties. Don't underestimate them. They are extremely skilled at what they do, and they have fooled some incredibly smart, experienced people.

Don't get me wrong, it is possible to create a successful Internet business. Many have done it – and you can be counted among them if you are careful and have the staying power to make it happen.

Two things to keep uppermost in your mind as you search for opportunities:

1. The establishment of a successful Internet business takes three things:

    → **TIME** - It will take at least a year (if you are extraordinarily lucky) and probably several years before you actually start making a substantial income.
    → **Seriously hard work** (several hours/day)
    → **Money** (Yes, I said money – most likely a minimum of $10,000).

2. Anyone who offers you an opportunity that is easy, painless, low-cost, and will generate a six-figure income in a few weeks is SCAMMING you!

Let's take a look at a couple of the fearsome bears that will be out to get you.

Establish an E-Mail Marketing Business

It is possible to build an Internet marketing business with a satisfying income stream by promoting products through e-mail. However, it is not nearly as easy as the bears who promote this type of business will make it sound.

Some of the basics that take time, knowledge, and energy to develop, which they neglect to mention are:

- Identifying a profitable niche.
- Finding a source for the product(s).
- Building a Website.
- Establishing your reputation as a credible retailer.
- Building a long list of loyal buyers and a second long list of potential buyers.

A saying you will hear often in this arena is, "The money is in the list." And – it is, which is why this scam tends to work.

They make you believe that they will give you a short-cut to developing those lists!

Always remember that when an advertisement promises that you can make a ton of money in a short time, they are ALWAYS selling something. In this case, they are typically selling a (useless) list of names and email addresses, which is how they are making their boatload of money.

There are so many problems with the lists they are selling that I don't know where to start, but the crucial one is: The CAN-SPAM Act.

In 2003, the United States Congress passed the CAN-SPAM Act. It became a law in January 2004. CAN-SPAM is an acronym.

Controlling the Assault
of Non-Solicited Pornography And Marketing.

The CAN-SPAM Act states that sending unsolicited bulk email is a crime. The Act is enforced by the Federal Trade Commission, and they do not take their responsibility lightly! If you violate the law, you are subject to fines and penalties handed down by the Department of Justice for up to $11,000 per incident. In other words, you cannot simply buy a list and start sending out e-mails, you could be found guilty of a crime.

As an example, one of the most common ways that legitimate internet marketers have built their lists is through what is known as an "opt-in" box on their Websites. Through these boxes (or other methods), people agree to have the merchants send email messages to them. Plus, every e-mail that is sent must have an "unsubscribe" link so that people can also opt-out whenever they choose to do so. If e-mail marketers follow these rules carefully and mail only to those who have given them permission to do so, the CAN-SPAM Act is not being violated when the marketers send out bulk e-mails.

When you buy a list of names and email addresses from anyone, you do not have permission to send bulk email to the names on that list. The really slick scam artists will tell you that they have the right to give you permission to send email to the names on the list, but that is a LIE – they do not have permission. Permission must be given by the owner of the email address to the person who will be sending the emails. There is no such thing as legitimate third party permission.

There are legitimate list-building techniques; but, they are not easy and they are certainly not fast. You can write and market e-books and articles, you can create your own Website with an opt-in box, and you can post to blogs and forums. You can do a lot of legal things to build your own legitimate opt-in list; but, you cannot BUY a legal opt-in list no matter who tells you that it is possible.

This is an enormous, stealthy bear that can cost you dearly. There are no shortcuts to building a successful online marketing business.

1-900 Business Opportunities

This is a big, bad and extremely nasty bear. The advertisement will read something like this: "Call 1-900-555-5555 to discover your pot of gold!!!!!"

There is nothing illegal about advertising a 900 number, but be aware that 900 number calls are not free. In fact, the cost per minute is set by the owner of the number and it can be ridiculously high, which means they've got you the minute you dial the number.

Charges begin immediately and can range from a few dollars to several dollars per minute. Of course, they will keep you talking as long as possible. They will give you information on how to set up your own 900 number and place advertisements to get others to call your 900 number. That is the big "secret" they are advertising that will create your "pot of gold."

Be sure to be sitting down when you open your next telephone bill because it will be exorbitant – possibly over $1,000 – and you will have no recourse. You must pay the bill or lose your telephone service.

You have probably already guessed that the person you called (the one who placed the ad) will receive most of the money that you pay to the telephone company.

NEVER call a 1-900 number!

There is no way to know what the charge per minute will be. And, the only secret you will get is how to scam others, just as you have been scammed.

Danger – Sneaky Snakes

There are definitely "lions and tigers and bears, oh my!" But the Internet Jungle is also populated with sneaky snakes. These creatures can sneak up and have your pocket picked before you know it.

Ponzi Schemes

One of the most popular ploys of the sneaky snakes is the Ponzi scheme, which is not always easy to identify. At first glance, it can appear to be a legitimate business; but first, a little history lesson to help you understand this ploy better.

Ponzi Schemes get their name from Charles Ponzi. He was born in Italy in 1882 and arrived in the United States in 1903. He was 21-years-old with only $2.50 in his pocket. But, what he had that was more significant was a boatload of ambition and a propensity for shady dealings. Ultimately, he managed to pull off one of the worst swindling schemes in history. It was so notorious that the swindle still bears his name…the Ponzi scheme.

As a prelude to the development of his infamous scheme, he stole money, got caught, and went to prison where he met a man by the name of Charles Morse. Mr. Morse convinced him that rich people can get away with almost anything; and from that point on, his primary goal in life was to become rich.

After he was released from prison, he married Rose Gnecco. He tried to make his fortune through several business ventures that all failed. The last legitimate effort was a catalog similar to what we know today as the yellow pages. It failed shortly after the campaign was launched; but, a few weeks later he received a letter from a company in Spain asking about the catalog. With the letter was a "postal coupon." The coupon was included so he could respond to the company in Spain (a foreign country) at no cost to himself. Ponzi saw an opportunity and turned the coupon into possibly the greatest extended scam in history.

The heart of the scheme was buying postal coupons in countries with low rates and cashing them in countries with high rates. It was a form of currency trading….which was, and still is, illegal. He claimed that, after expenses, he was making a 400% profit, which easily attracted investors into his scheme.

He made a lot of money quickly; but, was not happy with a small fortune. His greed took control. He convinced more and more investors to sink large sums into his company. He then used those funds to pay the former investors. The scheme was complicated, but remarkably effective. If you want to read all the details of the scheme, click here.

Charles Ponzi died in 1949; but, his name lives on in infamy….the scheme did not die with him.

Wikipedia defines a Ponzi scheme as, "A fraudulent investment operation that involves paying returns to investors out of the money raised from subsequent investors, rather than from profits generated by any real business. It offers high short-term returns in order to entice new investors, whose money is needed to fund payouts to earlier investors, and to lure its victims into ever-bigger risks." It was quite brilliant, but not brilliant enough to prevent his being caught, which happened eventually.

I think you can see why Ponzi schemes are classified as crimes of persuasion. People who are duped into investing in such schemes never go into them with any knowledge that their investment will allow a wicked few to profit from other people's misfortune. In fact, they would be horrified if they knew the truth about how their investments were going to be used. The investors are victims – not criminals.

A Ponzi scheme could be classified as an elaborate pyramid scheme because it never involves a real product. It only involves money.

Pyramid Schemes

Pyramid schemes, like Ponzi schemes, were not created by sneaky snakes on the Internet; they date back to the 1950's when chain letters became immensely popular.

Pyramid schemes that involve large sums of money are no longer sent through the United States Mail because that is now illegal. If caught, the perpetrators are fined heavily and sent to prison. Even if they were not illegal, most people are familiar enough with pyramid schemes that they would not be likely to participate in one.

Because they have been around forever and almost everyone has heard of them, it seems that they would be easily recognized. But, that is not always the case. The people who set them up today are talented scam artists who have found innovative ways to disguise them – and they are never, ever, labeled as pyramid schemes, which is why it is easy to get sucked in!

To protect yourself, it is essential to know how to identify them. These "opportunities" always come in unsolicited emails, so watch for the "buzz words" that are red flags and should trigger an immediate click of the DELETE button.

1. RECRUIT – The use of the word 'recruit' (or any synonym) should be a tip off that the program being promoted is most likely a pyramid scheme. Some of these schemes can be easily spotted while others are harder to identify. BEWARE when you see the word, "recruit" in any job promotion.

I was caught in one of these a couple of years ago through an unsolicited email. For only $300, I signed up to be a job recruiter and make a substantial income working only 20 hours a week. I fell for it! It seemed legitimate and a proper fit for my experience and skill set. I was so wrong. I not only lost the $300, but also lost all the money I spent trying to advertise my "job listings." After several weeks of working many hours each day and never earning a penny, I realized what was going on – I had been recruited, by someone who had been recruited, by someone who had been recruited, etc.; so, I quickly cut my losses and waved goodbye.

2. BUY THE SECRET and SELL . . . This offer is usually promoted as an 'exclusive' opportunity to buy a secret that will allow you to make a hundred thousand dollars a month (no work required). Then, you can sell this secret to others for a substantial profit, and they will make money for you. Seeing the promise in writing, it probably seems absurd that anyone would fall for it, but they do!

3. LET OTHERS DO THE WORK! This enticing phrase is always connected to a pyramid scheme. The sales pitch is usually for a non-existent product. For a fee, you will be sent a package by bulk mail with all the information you need to enlist others to promote the product; then, all you have to do is to sit back and let the money roll in. Does that sound too good to be true? Well, it is!

The hard truth of the matter is that there is no legitimate Internet business that will immediately make you hundreds of thousands of dollars a month. There is a slight chance that you will be able to make that kind of money through an Internet business ....someday – BUT, only after investing an incredible amount of time and effort in creating and building the business – and providing everything goes your way in the process.

Illegal MLMs

MLM (Multi-Level-Marketing) is similar in structure to a pyramid scheme, but it is not the same. In a full-blown pyramid scheme, there is no product. In MLM, there is an actual product.

Multi-level Marketing is defined as selling products by using independent distributors and allowing these distributors to build and manage their own sales force by recruiting, motivating, supplying, and training others to sell products. The distributors' compensation includes their own sales and a percentage of the sales of their sales group (their down line).

"So," you say, "that just sounds like a good idea for making money." Well, it IS an excellent way for making money. The problem is that many of them are illegal.

Do you see that tip-off word, 'recruiting'? The other tip-off that this is a MLM scheme is the phrase, 'percentage of sales'.

There is nothing illegal about setting up an affiliate program and PAYING a percentage of sales to those who sell your products or services to others. There is nothing illegal about COLLECTING the percentages that are offered by the producers of the products or services. That is simply smart business and a common practice in the Internet business world – a practice that can create a substantial income stream over a period of time with a lot of hard work.

The problem arises when a distributor COLLECTS a percentage of sales from people he has recruited to sell the product. Then another level is added and another and another – hence the term: multi-level marketing. Depending on how the company is structured, even one additional level can be illegal; but, more than five levels make the company suspect.

This is a business that you would be wise to avoid regardless of how good it sounds.

Characteristics that Make an MLM Illegal

In a report published by the FTC in 2006, they identified . . .

The Five Red Flags of product-based pyramid schemes, or recruiting MLM's:

1. Each person recruited is empowered and given incentives to recruit other participants, who are empowered and motivated to recruit still other participants, etc., creating an endless chain of empowered and motivated recruiters recruiting recruiters – without regard to (de facto) market saturation.

2. Advancement in a hierarchy of multiple levels of "distributors" is achieved by recruitment, rather than by appointment.

3. "Pay to play" requirements are met by ongoing "incentivized purchases," with participants the primary buyers.

4. The MLM company pays commissions and bonuses on more "distributor" levels than are functionally justified; i.e., more than five levels.

5. Company payout (in commissions, bonuses, etc.) per sale, for the total of all up line participants together, equals or exceeds that of the person selling the product – resulting in inadequate incentive to retail and excessive incentive to recruits.

PayPal Is the Watchdog

PayPal is the main Internet banking and money exchange. It employs full-time personnel to search for and identify illegal MLM schemes. When these schemes are uncovered, the account (and all attached accounts and credit cards) are frozen.

Occasionally PayPal will make a mistake and misidentify a legitimate business as a MLM scheme, but it doesn't happen often. When it does, the problem can usually be resolved in a few days.

The point is that there are those who are looking for illegal MLM schemes and if you involve yourself in one, you could suffer the consequences.

Recruiting Multi-level Marketing schemes have similarities to both Ponzi Schemes and pyramid schemes except that there is always a product involved in an MLM (Multi-Level Marketing). Ponzi, Pyramid, and Recruiting MLM schemes are all illegal!

The people who promote these schemes are some of the sneakiest snakes that live and thrive on the Internet, but they aren't the only variety of snakes.

When you are active on the Internet - especially when you are doing business - you are extremely visible to your suppliers, your customers, your potential customers, and to all the sneaky snakes that will do everything possible to take your money.

As we explained, the rules and regulations of the CAN-SPAM Act are terribly strict; but, that doesn't mean that the spammers have all gone away. There are laws against robbing convenience stores, as well; but, the robberies continue and so does SPAM. There will always be people who knowingly break the law to make money.

Always err on the side of caution.
Be safe, rather than sorry!

CHAPTER 3

OFFERS OF HELP

Danger – Not-so-Friendly Natives

Hopefully, by now you have a greater awareness of creatures in the Internet Jungle who will happily take your money, make your life miserable, and ultimately rob you of your dreams if you let them.

In addition to the dangerous animals, there are some natives who are not-so-friendly. In fact, they are as dangerous as the animals because of their trapping expertise. Among their most effective traps are those that are baited with the offer of help – an offer that few newbies in the jungle can resist.

As you read through the following list, you may think to yourself, "I would never fall for any of these scams." I understand the reaction because reading them in this context; they will probably seem obvious.

However, the words, "Let us HELP you" are music to the ears of people who have invested a lot of time and energy searching for a viable, legitimate home-based business with no success. A seemingly endless search can put anyone (including you) in such a desperate frame of mind that the temptation to reach for an offer that can lighten your load and make the process easier is almost impossible to resist. Be careful, the offers of help are rarely (if ever) what they seem. They are well-set traps.

Let's look at the way the offers are framed and study some of the key words and phrases that should be red flags that are warning you to stay away. Hopefully, this review will help you instantly recognize the scams – and pushing the delete key will become an automatic response when you see one.

All of the following headlines imply an offer of help and are forms of pure Internet scam baiting.

You have been CHOSEN

Who can resist opening a message with the headline like this? This enticing little bait shows up in your inbox unsolicited, which makes it spam, of course – but the word "chosen" may pull you in.

The message will begin with something like, "You have been chosen to participate in a_____!" The blank can be filled in many ways. The reality is that the only thing you have been chosen for is to be scammed by the perpetrators and to lose any money you are willing to give them. Do not fall for this one!

You are SO SMART!

This is particularly effective bait because it is designed to make you believe that FINALLY somebody realizes just how smart you truly are.

These messages generally arrive in your email box – unsolicited. When you see anything resembling that statement, you can be assured that it is SPAM. The offer usually goes on to say that because you are such an intelligent person, you can become an Internet Consultant and earn millions just by advising others. These types of advertisements also pop up on Websites, as well, which does not make them any more legitimate.

For anyone new to the world of Internet commerce, critical questions should come to mind: What do you know about a field that you have just begun to explore? How could you possibly be a consultant? What advice do you have to give? All valid questions; but, the not-so-friendly native that baited this trap is ready and willing to tell you everything you need to know (to train you) so that you can become a highly paid and sought after "consultant".....for a price, of course!

You are SO HONEST!

Of course, you are honest! You have always known that you were honest, but it is rare that anyone else makes such a blatant statement about your honesty. You know they don't know you, and it is obvious that they are selling something – but, this bait is usually an offer for a credit card or guaranteed loan to help you start your business (a little different slant).

This advertisement is often sent through an unsolicited email, but you may also see these types in trade magazines and in newspapers. Don't let that fool you, they are still scams.

The pitch is that even if you are young and not well established financially; or, even if you have had credit difficulties in the past, they know that you are an honest person, and they are willing to help you. You may be offered a home equity loan even if you don't have any equity, or a high-limit credit card no matter what your credit is – because you are so honest. The big warning sign on this one is when you see the word 'honest' repeated multiple times in one advertisement.

If you are trying to start a business on a shoe string, this particular bait may hook you.

You DESERVE our help!

One of the things that most people struggle with is the belief that they are somehow undeserving of the best things that life has to offer. Yet, somewhere deep inside, there is always a quiet little voice telling you that you do deserve the best. This is just human nature and can be used against you as bait by the Not-so-Friendly Natives to lure unsuspecting innocents into their traps. You want help, and they are offering it.

This bait comes in many disguises. It can be used to lure you into making risky investments for quick returns, to establish off-shore bank accounts, or buy land in foreign countries. My advice is to delete them immediately because they are usually Ponzi Schemes or they are an attempt to get your personal information to steal your identity.

Some offers are for free goods and services, or membership in a "buying club," which is a tricky one because there are many legitimate buying clubs that offer substantial discounts on brand name merchandize. The difference is that the legitimate buying club offers do not arrive in your inbox as unsolicited mail.

Success can be EASY!

Everybody hopes to find the easy way to be successful. Even though most of us are willing to put forth the necessary time and effort, there is always the lazy side (and we all have it) that would like to do as little as possible to achieve our goals. For that reason, bait that promises easy success is extremely tempting.

These advertisements sometimes arrive as unsolicited mail in your inbox; but, they can also be found all over the Internet, plus in newspapers and magazines, even direct mail. Easy riches – WOW! That is terribly hard to ignore.

They tell you that only fools work hard for their money because, in reality making money is so easy that it is essentially a no-brainer. Their message is that hard work is overrated and an unnecessary burden. Then, they offer you the "secret" to making millions while doing as little as possible – for an amazingly low price.

There are people who have so much money that they do not have to work, but they were born into wealth, inherited hundreds of thousands or millions, or they hit the lottery (which means they won't have it for long). Another hard cold truth is that you have a better chance of being struck by lightning than you have of making millions without working.

This bait is designed to make the conniving natives rich by taking money out of your pocket and putting it into their pockets while they work as little as possible in the process.

You can learn the SECRETS of Success!

The "secrets of success" implies powerful information that is not common knowledge. This bait appeals to your desire to be among the few who are privy to such valuable information! Who doesn't want to know the secrets of success?

The Internet Jungle is fertile ground for the not-so-friendly natives who want to sell you "secrets." Once your name is out there, you will be inundated with offers. You may get three-four-five per day urging you to buy their book, sign up for a training course, or webinar that will give you the secrets that "helped them or one of their students make six figures in only 10 days" (or - something similar).

Some courses and seminars will provide useful information for novice Internet entrepreneurs; but, the information is not secret. The information can range from bits of wisdom and expert advice to helpful nuggets of knowledge gained through personal experience.

You can learn a lot from those who have blazed trails. The authentic ones have hard-earned wisdom they can share....but, nothing they tell you is secret. The information they will be giving you is all over the Internet, they have simply packaged it in a way that may be beneficial to you, or not.

The problem is that anyone can offer secrets of success; but, that does not mean that every offer made is coming from a successful Internet marketer. The challenge is finding a way to sift through all of the offerings and to decide which courses, seminars, teleseminars, or webinars are valid and will actually benefit you.

Always investigate the people making the offering. Are they genuinely who they say they are, or are they just jungle beasts ready to pounce and take your money?

Find out who is offering the course and the names of the speakers on the Webinar who will be offering you a product with their money-making secrets. (Both will be cashing in on the money you pay if they get you.)

Search names on Google, Bing and Yahoo – see what comes up. Read as much as you can, including Page 2 and Page 3 listings. The first entries may be the trapper's own hype. You need to dig deeper to see everything that is being said.

Make sure you are well-informed before you pay for the information they are offering. The "opportunity to purchase" will be there tomorrow. Don't take this bait without knowing exactly whom you are dealing with!

You can learn to SELL Anything!

Robert Louis Stevenson, Scottish novelist and poet (1850-1894) wrote, "Everyone lives by selling something." How true! We all sell something. We sell our time, our knowledge, a product, or a service. Everybody is selling something and some of us do it better than others.

There are effective selling techniques that you can learn; but, to be successful at selling, you must have something of value to sell in order to attract paying customers. Pure hype won't cut it, at least not for long.

Selling is only half of the sales process. The other half of the process is the customer. The seller must meet and exceed customer expectations or business will not be sustainable. If customers are not happy, they can complain and/or ask for a refund. If you sell inferior products, returns and refunds will mount up. Your credibility and reputation will be severely damaged.

You can learn to be an expert salesperson; and, selling a quality product or service will help to guarantee that it will stay sold. Regardless of the headline, you have to sell something of value to be successful. You cannot learn to sell *anything* (nor would you want to sell inferior products or services).

Summary

As you read through the different types of common bait used by the trappers to get you in their clutches, you probably recognized some, or even all of them. You may be an educated, savvy business person with years of experience and believe that you are too smart to be caught in such traps. I certainly hope that is true.

I thought that I was too smart to be caught; but, as much as I hate to admit it, the not-so-friendly-natives caught me several times last year. Later I will share with you my views on Webinars and training offered by the EXPERTS. But, for now I want to tell you about one of the slickest ones that caught me.

The offer did not come through my e-mail; it came as a personalized letter in the mail, which made it feel more legitimate.

I had been chosen because of my unique talents and abilities that made me an ideal candidate for membership in their select group. Their sales pitch was so slick that I was a goner after reading the first page. There was also a strong element of urgency built into the offer. I had to make a decision by a certain date, or lose the opportunity forever. The worst part is that I didn't come to my senses until three letters later over a period of three months and an investment of $400.

Really naïve and foolish – right? Absolutely; but, I desperately NEEDED some guidance and help in reaching the level of success that I wanted. I thought they were going to give me the *secrets to success.* You can laugh if you want to. I would laugh with you if it didn't still hurt when I think about it.

My goal in writing this book is to help others be better informed than I was. I want you to make wiser decisions regarding how you invest your money in the entrepreneurial adventure of finding a legitimate business on the Internet. I want you to be successful and to realize your dream with less pain than I had to endure.

Danger – Friendly Natives
Who Make Wild Promises

HELLO, I AM...

GOING TO MAKE YOU RICH!

There are hundreds of "friendly natives" who will make outlandish promises that are impossible to keep – and should be recognized for what they are. DO NOT BELIEVE THEM – no matter how much you want to. If you accept what they say and make the mistake of buying from them, don't say you weren't warned.

These are probably the most difficult to resist, because the marketers tell such a good story. Unfortunately, most of it is pure hype. The chances of succeeding to the level they promise is practically "0".

There is the possibility that there may be one or two that will work. If you do everything they ask, step-by-step with great focus and persistence, never faltering for a second, you may end up make the millions promised.

However, an extremely high percentage of people who "buy" never follow through – and never complain. That is what they are counting on – and exactly how the make their millions.

For the most part, these programs do not come cheap! So be very cautious

Make $100,000 a MONTH with a fool-proof money-making system.

The story these "Internet Gurus" tell is that they started with nothing. Then, after years of work and research they finally found the secret or developed the system that has made them rich and now they want to share it with you.

Remember… anybody can CLAIM anything as a fact. It is easy to slip past the Truth in Advertising Act in the Internet Marketing Jungle.

Stop and think for a minute. If someone were making $100,000 each and every month with their fool-proof, money-making system, why would they be willing to teach you (and anyone else who is willing to pay) how to compete with them?

If you had found out how to find the pot of gold at the end of every rainbow, would you sell that information at any price? I don't think so.

Instant Riches Can Be Yours!

This wild promise comes in a wide variety of disguises. The offer made in the advertisement changes from month to month and from year to year, but the message is always the same.

These are the friendly natives that are preying on your ambition. The message promises unbelievable wealth overnight – all you need to do is learn how to make it.

Here is the hard, cold truth: You can be a successful online business entrepreneur – IF and ONLY IF you are willing to invest the time, energy, and money that are required to become successful.

Once you have made it, it may seem like overnight to your family and friends, but you will know the truth about the money you spent, the long hours you put in, the frustration and disappointments you suffered, and the extremely hard work that was required to make you an overnight success.

Regardless of how convincing any sales pitch may be, repeat to yourself the following mantra, "Fortunes are never made overnight. They are the result of hard work, dedication, and an unwavering focus on your goals."

Write Articles for Cash

If someone promises to teach you how to write 300- to 400-word articles that you can sell for $1,000/each, run away as fast as you can (don't walk). This person is not a friendly native.

If you bite, you will pay a lot of money for a secret that doesn't exist. Even if you are a talented writer, you would have to write 200 articles at $5.00/each in order to make a $1,000 . . . and that is if you know the rules of Internet article writing and are extremely lucky.

Become a Blogging Millionaire

When this friendly native first appeared, my reaction was, "You have to be kidding!" I laughed, shook my head in disbelief and was convinced that no one would buy into this scheme. Unfortunately, I was dead wrong.

There are many variations of this scam. One pitch is: "Set up a blog (which you can do at no cost) and sell high-priced advertising space to big companies that have stacks of advertising dollars lying around waiting for you to claim it."

Internet blogs are extremely popular, but you will not make millions by simply starting your own blog. A blog is a tool used by many Internet marketers, but it is not a viable business by itself, unless you are famous or infamous enough to draw hordes of traffic, making it a good place for companies to advertise.

You can be guaranteed that whoever is doing the advertising of such offers is NOT doing it for your benefit. They are selling something that will make money for THEM – not YOU.

The blog may be free, but they will make you believe that their training program, which may range in price from $97.00 up to $997.00, will give you everything you need to know to turn your blog into a money-making machine.

I have no idea how many blogs there are on the Internet, but there are many! If you stop and think about this for a minute, you know as well as I do that large corporations are not going to pay you for advertising on your little Website blog.

Fact: 99.9% of the bloggers on the Internet will NEVER make millions (or even thousands) selling advertising space on their blogs.

Get to #1 in Google Search Results

If you have been on the Internet for a while and have purchased anything, it is almost a certainty that you have received e-mails promoting seminars or courses that include a statement that goes something like this, "Learn how to get the number one spot in Google search results!" Don't you believe it!

Advertising in any form is always about manipulation through words and how they are cleverly put together to get you to do what they want. If you analyze the statement, they are not promising that you will actually get to the number one spot in Google search results….only that they will TEACH you how to get the number one spot in Google search results. If you don't get there . . . it's on you – not them.

I can teach you how to get the #1 spot right now, in one sentence: Get more traffic and links to your Webpage than all your competitors on the Internet. That is the secret – simple, right? WRONG! The challenge is HOW to get more traffic and HOW to get more links to your website than everyone else on the Internet who is offering the same types of products or services. The devil is always in the details….those pesky little details!

There are many tried and true techniques to raise your PR (Page Rank); but, even when you have learned the techniques and diligently apply them month after month, getting ranked #1 and staying there is extremely difficult. Everyone wants to do that – and only a few actually succeed.

Any place on the first page of Google is practically sacred ground. No one – absolutely NO ONE – will ever fulfill a guarantee to make YOU number one. Don't buy into that wild promise. Reaching that hallowed first page takes time, hard work, and patience.

As I said before, there are many tried and true techniques to raise your PR. It is important to learn them and to apply them in order to increase your visibility on the Internet.

The thing the gurus do not tell you is that information on the best techniques is actually free on the Internet if you are willing to look for it.

The problem is that with today's social mentality of "I want it NOW," the majority of people do not want to take the time to dig it out for themselves. If that is your mindset and you are unwilling to take the time or lack the patience to seek out the free information, there are many books and e-books available that can help you.

You can also buy a training course; or, attend seminars, teleseminars, or webinars that are offered by legitimate gurus on almost every subject. With their guidance (if you follow through and do the work), you can raise your visibility and page ranking; and possibly, even make it to page one on Google. BUT, choose the gurus carefully – if they are legitimate, they will not guarantee to get you to #1 on Google. They will only provide the tools. The rest is up to you.

Lucrative Joint Venture Deals

This is another wild promise that some fake Internet gurus will make. "I will teach you how to get lucrative joint-venture deals!" The reason this one works is that there are lucrative joint-venture deals to be had on the Internet. But…the chance of an "unknown newbie" getting one is another story.

High search engine rankings and smart joint ventures are two favorites in the Internet Jungle. They are the gold rings….that everyone wants to grab.

Joint ventures are absolutely possible, but finding one is at the same level of difficulty as catching that golden ring on the merry-go-round when you were a child. It can be done; but, you have to prepare for the opportunity with a lot of stretching and practice.

The phrase, joint venture, causes well-established Internet marketers as well as brand new Internet marketers to get all excited. It is common knowledge that a joint venture is probably the fastest and easiest way to build a large opt-in list, to get established or become better established in the Internet Jungle, and to make a lot of money

But, let's be practical and look at the cold, hard facts. To attract an established Internet marketer with a substantial list, you would have to be willing to give him/her 100% of the profit on a product that you developed or had someone develop for you – and the market value would have to be at least $100. It is likely that the only thing that you would gain from your initial joint venture is a much larger opt-in list of your own. If you haven't heard it yet, you will hear it often, "The money is in the list" – so that particular gain is very, VERY valuable; but, the bank won't credit it to your account.

If you work hard, educate yourself, follow the rules, pay your dues, learn how to approach established Internet marketers, understand the legalities of joint venture agreements, etc., you may have the opportunity to land a lucrative joint venture – eventually. Or, even better, you may become a well-established marketer that others seek out and willingly give you 100% of their profits.

But, neither of those is going to happen today…next week…or even next year, unless….you are incredibly smart, you develop an amazing product, you have a phenomenal work ethic, you do everything right, you have laser focus with no distractions, you have no fear, you go after it with the tenacity of a bulldog, and are very, VERY lucky….even then, there is no guarantee.

Avoid Shortcuts to Success

Shortcuts can be amazing when they work. If they are well-traveled and time-tested, they are invaluable. But, in my experience, shortcuts often end up taking more time and costing more money in the long run than if I had taken a well-traveled path.

The friendly natives love selling shortcuts because they know it is extremely easy to literally "cash in" with them. The shortcuts they are offering are nothing more than a different set of wild promises that you must ignore.

Buying Lists

One common shortcut that is offered by fake Internet gurus is – how to build an opt-in list with very little work. They will lead you to believe that it is not necessary to offer an incentive to people, or write and market articles and e-books, or write regular posts for a blog, or actively participate in forums. They say, "There is an easier way....which I can show you. For a small price you can begin building your list NOW!"

Since you have probably already learned that building an opt-in list really does involve a lot of patience and hard work, you may be very tempted to take the shortcut that they are offering. This is my advice: DO NOT go down that road. There is about a 99.9% chance that the shortcut they will show you, for that very small price, is how to BUY a list.

Advertisements are everywhere for companies who will sell you an opt-in list that they claim contains names and email addresses of people who have already opted in....some of them are double opt-ins.

The list will cost you anywhere from $.03 per name and e-mail address up to $.30 each. According to those who are selling the lists, the price depends on whether the list contains names and addresses that are of the single opt-in variety or the double opt-in variety.

This offer has a lot of emotional appeal; but, my advice is to take a giant step backward and think about what you would be buying.

Opt-in lists are names and email addresses of real people – like you and me. Does it make any sense that individuals would deliberately provide their names and email addresses for the purpose of being put on a list that would be sold to anyone who is willing to pay for it? I certainly wouldn't do it and I am sure you wouldn't do it either.

With the escalating problem of identity theft and the social awareness of the dangers involved, people do not readily give out their names and email addresses so that the information can be sold. The fact is that there is absolutely no such thing as a legitimate opt-in list that you can buy. Even if the people on the list did opt-in to some list – they didn't opt-in to your list. If you send e-mails to people who have not given you permission to do so, you could be found guilty of violating the CAN-SPAM Act and face a serious fine.

Article Submission Software

Another shortcut that you may be offered by these fake Internet Gurus is automated article submission software. If you have not yet attempted to write and submit articles to article banks, you should know that it is incredibly time consuming. As a result, it can be very tempting to look for a shortcut to this process.

Bulk article submission was a tactic that worked until the end of 2012, when Google, Yahoo and MSN developed search algorithms that have a much greater emphasis on trust and usage data. As a result of those changes, article submission sites are no longer very effective for search engine rankings. If you were to put it to the test, you would find that only 5% of the major article sites can help you very much with page rank – the other 95% of article submission sites will do nothing for you.

I do not want to discourage you from using article marketing as one of your strategies. There are some very good legitimate forms of article marketing such as: guest blogging or guest authorship, and guest writing, plus quality article submission sites such as Ezine Articles, Buzzle, Go Articles, and Article Dashboard.

(Side note: Ezine Articles will not allow you to publish an article on their site that has been published anywhere else on the Internet – and they always check.)

Unfortunately, article marketing has been tainted by an ever-increasing number of poorly-written articles being submitted and then re-submitted through article spinning and article republishing – all of which has been encouraged by the promoters of bad article submission software. Let me give you an example:

Johnny Smith decides that he is going to use article marketing to drive traffic to his new Website. He sits down and writes a rather useless, poorly written article about pet sitting and includes links back to his "Pet Care" Website, which he is trying to get ranked. He decides that instead of just publishing the article on his site, he will submit it to a lot of article directories, article portals, article resource sites, article publishers – or whatever they are calling them these days. But, to make it easier on himself, he purchases an article spinning software for only $299, which will submit his article to all these different places for him.

There are many others like this young man who are glutting the market with trash and making it more difficult for talented writers to get their work noticed; but, the biggest problem with using automated article submission software – even for talented writers – is that most of the major banks and repositories will not accept submissions that are made with such software. They require that each submission be made by hand and individually posted in order for them to be listed on their sites.

Below are four good reasons why article submission for Search Engine Optimization (SEO) is not a very productive link-building tactic and why my recommendation is to publish your best articles on your own Website rather than posting them on article sites.

1. Most article sites are not trusted by the search engines, so the chance of getting any real juice from links that you acquire is nil.
2. If you publish an article on an article site and promote on Facebook, Twitter, etc., the links will go back to the article site – not to your site
3. Any links back to the article from other Websites – will (again) be back to the article site – not to your site.
4. Any search engine traffic that does result from the article will go to the article site. And, even though your link is in the article, readers may or may not click on it (probably won't).

If you have a great article, you want your readers (followers) to see it – and any juice that flows from it to come to you rather than go to someone else. The bottom line is – keep the good stuff at home.

Publishing your work on article sites in addition to your own Website, is not worth the time and effort because article sites rarely generate much traffic (even the good sites) – and only one copy of an article will be counted by search engines.

Publishing good, informative articles on your own Website and marketing them through press releases and social media, etc. is a proven SEO tactic – use it!

FFA's (Free for All)

It seemed important to mention this shortcut even though it is not as prevalent as it once was just in case it shows up on your radar. The short cut is: FFA Pages.

I should explain what FFA means (and it is not Future Farmers of America). It means "Free for All" Websites – also known as FFA Pages. At first, they appear harmless because they are presented as bulletin boards on which you can post your link or place an advertisement for your Website (similar to classified ads). The spiel is that others will visit, be impressed, and go to your Website. Free advertising sounds really good when you are just getting started on the Internet (or anytime for that matter), but all is not what it seems – don't believe anything these promoters tell you.

This is particularly appealing to inexperienced new owners of websites who are desperate for traffic. They are willing to try everything and anything to develop a presence on the Internet. Many newbies have been caught in this tricky little trap. They are seduced into thinking that it is free exposure for their Websites – so why not? Unfortunately, the only real exposure they get is a flood of unsolicited e-mails (SPAM) – by the ton.

The spam that results from a listing on an FFA page can be so heavy that you may even be forced to close down the e-mail address that you used, which will then result in many lost hours notifying personal friends, companies, and professional contacts that your e-mail address has changed.

One man tells the following story:

> About 10 days ago, I decided to try an FFA site and posted a link to my Website, using one of my regular email addresses. In my naiveté, I thought that the worst thing that could happen was that I would receive a few advertisements from other businesses. After the first few hundred advertisements showed up, I followed the FFA Page's instructions on the Remove/Ban procedure. That was a joke . . . because I continued to receive hundreds of more advertisements. The operator of the FFA site was completely unsympathetic, so I contacted the ISP that was hosting it – no luck there either. Their stance was that by posting a link on the site, I had agreed to receive all the advertisements. The only thing the remove/ban link did was to prevent me from making any future submissions, but did nothing to stop the advertisements.

There are many other similar stories from users who have been caught in this trap and struggled to get loose. My recommendation is to avoid FFA's like the plague. Regardless of what they tell you, their purpose is not to support you in your effort to build traffic for your Website. They have one goal and that is to collect e-mail addresses that can be sold.

If you should choose to take the risk, it is like shouting to the virtual world, "I LOVE SPAM – sock it to me!" You will have opted into a list that will fill up your inbox to overflowing everyday well into the future, or until – out of desperation – you change your e-mail address to make it stop.

Software Scams

The Not-so-Friendly Natives are everywhere with their Internet software scams – masterfully disguised as legitimate products.

They know that it is unlikely that the Newbies will ask the right questions (or any questions for that matter) before being convinced that the software offering is the answer to their prayers. And, they will buy immediately because it is only available "at this price" for the next 24 hours.

If you are not careful, you will end up in the same situation I was in – trapped by my desire to find the silver bullet (software program) that would make me instantly successful. I continued to buy into the promises that "this software would be the one!" I wanted to believe them, so I did. Unfortunately, most Newbies are often just as gullible as I was and quickly become software junkies.

As a Newbie, the quicker you recognize your addiction and find a way to control it, the better. For as long as it has you in its clutches, you are not only perfect prey for the Cannibals, you will spend far more money than necessary (or than you can afford), and you will end up with a ton of **T.U.S.**

Totally Useless Software.

Don't put yourself in the position of dreading the day when you must finally take the time to delete the hundreds of files and programs that you purchased while under the influence!

When a scammer promises that a piece of software will lighten your work load, create the perfect never-fail advertisement, or simplify the marketing process; the Newbie will almost always buy! The scammers are well aware of this. In fact....they depend on it.

Bogus, Stolen, or Legitimate

When you are on a tight budget, bargains are immensely appealing, and deep discounts always get your attention. This is another thing that the Cannibals understand and use against you.

Popular and useful programs such as Adobe Photoshop and Microsoft Word are some of the brand names used in this scam. If you see these types of products at incredibly low prices – BEWARE – there is a chance that they are pirated.

It is illegal to sell pirated software; but, it is equally illegal to buy pirated software if there were any indication that the product you bought was pirated. Prices well-below the market are BIG red flags and should make you run the other way.

Checklist – Legal or Illegal?

→ Check the price of the software on the manufacturer's Website. If the selling price is way out of line with the manufacturer's list price, do not go anywhere near it.

→ All legitimate software manufacturers and retailers will give you a written warranty. They will also have a fair refund policy. Cannibals will not offer either one.

→ Manufacturers of legitimate software embed code in the software, which is printed on the packaging; or the code is sent via e-mail if sold electronically. It is usually a 30-digit number, which is used to activate the software. It is called the *Product Key*. It contains information about the software and provides mechanisms to validate and activate the product, emitting a signed Product License only for the machine that activated the product. If you are instructed to activate the software in any other way – the software is probably stolen or pirated.

→ If you see NFR or OEM printed on an install disk, the software was stolen. NFR means, Not for Resale and is usually stamped on a beta product version. OEM means Original Equipment Manufacturer, which is stamped on software that is included in the purchase of a new computer.

→ All legitimate software can be registered. If the seller of the software tells you that it cannot be registered, you can bet that it was stolen. Once again, if you buy software that you know has been stolen, that is a criminal act. Receiving stolen property is a crime in all fifty states and most civilized countries in the world. Don't do it!

→ Legitimate software suppliers will always provide their names, addresses and telephone numbers. Those selling stolen or pirated software will provide you with names, addresses, and telephone numbers, as well.... but they will be fake; and their email addresses are changed daily...or more frequently.

→ Bulk email and the CAN-SPAM Act were discussed in a previous section. Legitimate software manufacturers and retailers do not engage in the illegal act of sending bulk mailing (SPAM). If you receive a software offer through SPAM mail – delete immediately, even if it is the best price you have ever seen – don't even think about it.

Yes, you will need some software. You can't work on the Internet without it. Obviously, you need the basics like Microsoft Word, possibly Excel, and Adobe Photoshop – or similar programs. You do not need all the bells and whistles to begin and Open Office (which is free) works pretty well in place of Word. Shop around. There are free versions of almost every type of software that you will need.

Don't spend money you do not need to spend and don't overload your computer with unnecessary software and extra features that you will probably never use. It is excess baggage, which will drain resources from your computer and slow it down.

Participate in forums, you will be amazed at all the valuable tips you will pick up regarding free products; and if you must buy, participants in the forum can help you learn what to buy, where to buy and what to avoid. If you purchase software, purchase it from the manufacturer, or legitimate retailers. Bargain hunting for these products may cost you far more than you will save

Three questions to answer honestly before you purchase any software:

- ***Do I really need this software?*** This is often the hardest one to answer because it is easy to confuse want and need. If the software will absolutely help you work faster and make your job a lot easier, then it may be a wise choice. But, you must evaluate it carefully. Wishing will not make it so. If it is just going to take up resources on your computer and slow it down without providing any real benefits for you, then it is TUS (Totally Useless Software). Look at the features, if it is bloated with features you will never use, look for a more basic model, possibly an older version.

- ***Is the asking price in line with the manufacturers' or legitimate retailers' asking price?*** If it is not, it is either bogus or you could be buying stolen goods, which is a crime. (Do I sound like a broken record?) Be as wary as you would be with a street vendor in New York City who tries to sell you a Rolex for $29.95. You would know immediately that it was either a knock off, or stolen – neither of which would be a wise purchase.

- ***Is there a money-back guarantee with a reasonable time limit?*** Never buy software that does not come with a guarantee that covers both the product and its functionality on your computer.

To sum it all up – if you want to manage a business on the Internet, you need a certain amount of software – without it, your computer is useless – with it, you can be creative and productive. BUT… in the beginning you only need the basics – you do not need all the bells and whistles – DO NOT let the Scammer get you.

If you do succumb to the temptation and order software from scam artists, pay for it, and it never shows up – or you don't receive download instructions immediately, believe it or not – that is the best of the worst things that can happen to you.

The Not-so-Friendly Natives have found that selling bogus software or stolen software is an easy way to catch and gobble up their prey. If the software is delivered as promised, it may contain malicious codes for the purpose of phishing or pharming – which is explained in the next chapter.

CHAPTER 4

IDENTITY THEFT

Danger – The Cannibals

After you have been in the Internet Jungle for a while, searching for work-at-home opportunities, and ventured far enough into the depths to have encountered and successfully survived attacks from lions, tigers, bears, and sneaky snakes, the next thing you have to worry about are the cannibals who will eat you alive. (OMG!)

The more you use the Internet, the more vulnerable you become. As you diligently scour the Web for business opportunities or ways to develop your skills in Internet marketing, etc. the Cannibals are watching and waiting. The only thing you can count on is that they will come after you.

The worst part about a Cannibal is that s/he looks, speaks and acts just like any other normal Internet business person. Every cannibal is on the lookout for innocent, hardworking, unsuspecting newbies on the Internet because they are much easier marks than those who have been living in the Internet Jungle for a while – and are more wary.

Phishing and Pharming

Both of these illegal practices are used by the Internet Cannibals and are extremely dangerous. They are designed to rob you of your personal information or to hack into your Website, and then to use the information in a multitude of criminal ways.

Both words are probably familiar; but, if you do not know exactly what they mean, it is time to lean.

PHISHING

A phishing expedition, like a fishing expedition, is a speculative venture: the phisher drops the lure into the Internet and hopes to reel in as many fish as possible. The primary purpose of phishing is online identity theft.

It is an online con game run by tech-savvy con artists (AKA Cannibals). Using a variety of methods, the phisher lures you into providing your personal financial information on a fraudulent web site, also known as a spoofed web site.

Phishing is e-mail fraud in which the perpetrator sends out legitimate-looking e-mails that appear to come from well-known and trustworthy Web sites such as a business or organization that you deal with (your bank, an online payment service such as PayPal, an auction house such as eBay, your Internet service provider (ISP), or even a government agency). The message usually says that you need to "update" or "validate" your account information, and often threatens the closure of your account if you don't respond – and a link is provided.

When clicked, the email link will take you to an official-looking web site, which usually looks identical to the real one (since the perpetrator has simply lifted the logos and wording from the real site), and will request you to enter your account number, password, etc.

If you are not alert to this type of phishing expedition, you may simply follow the instructions and enter your information because the site looks so real. The phisher immediately steals your personal data and can use it to clean out your bank accounts or commit other criminal acts tied to identity theft.

The best protection from all phishing scams is to never, EVER click on a link in an email from an unknown or suspicious e-mail address. If you are not sure whether it is phishing, or not, go directly to the known legitimate Website and ask the company about the request.

I have received a number of these emails using an exact copy of my bank's website that looked so authentic that when I received the first one, I had to stop and think about it. The only reason I hesitated and didn't follow the directions immediately was because the message didn't make sense to me. Fortunately, I checked with my bank and was told that it was a phishing scheme.

Big reliable sites have been fooled by these scams…and you could be fooled, as well, if you are not careful.

Whenever you receive a message that is even slightly suspicious and could be phishing, you should do the following:

- **DELETE IT immediately without hesitation!** (This is the best choice)

- **NEVER REPLY!** If you reply – your "from address" will be used to harvest a list of working email addresses which the spammer can use to optimize his or her operations.

- **BEWARE of e-mail that automatically loads images.** Spammers can encode your email address in the URL used to retrieve images.

- **NEVER buy anything from a spammer.**

- **NEVER click links in an email from a source you do not recognize.** Even if you do recognize the "sender's email address" be careful, it could be a forged e-mail address. If the message seems strange in any way, delete it.

PHARMING

This is similar to phishing, but more sophisticated and harder to detect. Even though pharmers also work through emails, there is no attachment to open. Your financial information can be compromised by simply opening the email message.

Security Search describes it as follows:

"Pharming is a scamming practice in which malicious code is installed on a personal computer or server, misdirecting users to fraudulent Web sites without their knowledge or consent. Pharming has been called "phishing without a lure."

The Cannibals hijack a legitimate Website's domain name and URL. Then, they send an email message, which they are fairly certain you will open when you recognize the sender. The problem is that the message contains a virus that installs a small software program on your computer. The next time you try to visit the official website, you will be sent to the pharmer's fake version of the web site, where he can capture your personal financial information that you enter – and once again, he will use it as he pleases.

The newest and the worst kind of pharming requires no email at all. You may be attacked without even knowing it. These Cannibals use keystroke loggers that capture account names and passwords, which they can use for future fraudulent transactions.

Now that you are aware of the dangers, take the following steps as protection against phishers and pharmers:

→ Check with your bank to see if they have any protective software implemented that will thwart the efforts of these Cannibals.

→ Always maintain an effective, up-to-date virus protection and Internet security such as Norton AntiVirus™ and Norton Internet Security™, which blocks suspicious Web sites automatically. It doesn't catch everything, but almost everything; and you can breathe a little easier with this protection.

- Staples has a product (Sophos) that provides even greater protection than Norton, but it is more costly.
- My recommendation is to stay away from McAfee. Once it is on your computer it is almost impossible to remove – and it can mess up your system. Also, be careful if you choose to use it because it may have other offers that piggy-back on the download. Be sure to read and check or uncheck all the boxes that are connected with any download.

→ Make sure your browser is up-to-date and security patches are applied.

→ Use a trusted, legitimate Internet Service Provider with rigorous security at the ISP level. This is your first line of defense against pharming.

→ Check the URL of any site that asks you to provide personal information. Make sure your session begins at the known authentic address of the official site, with no extra characters appended to it.

→ Check the certificate, which takes only a few seconds, to see if the site you land on is legitimate. For example, on the latest version of Internet Explorer, go to "File" in the main menu and select "Properties." When the box pops up, click on "Certificates" and check to see if the site carries a secure certificate from its legitimate owner.

→ Be suspicious of any email with urgent requests for personal financial information and delete immediately.

→ Never use links to get to any web page if the message is from an unknown sender.

→ Never complete forms in email messages that ask for personal financial information.

→ Always verify that a Web site is secure when submitting credit card or other sensitive information via the web browser. (This is one reason that I use PayPal as much as possible.)

→ Consider installing a web browser tool bar for protection from known phishing fraud web sites.

→ Regularly check bank, credit card, and debit card statements to ensure all transactions are legitimate. (At least twice a month)

→ Never allow yourself to be pressured into providing sensitive information.

If you suspect that you have been a victim of phishing or pharming, take the following steps:

1. Forward the entire original email to the Federal Trade Commission at spam@uce.gov (not sure this helps, but worth a try).
2. Forward the email to the "abuse" email address at the company that is being spoofed (e.g. spoof@WellsFargoBank.com)
3. Notify the Internet Fraud Complaint Center (IFCC) of the FBI by filing a complaint on the IFCC's web site: http://www.ic3.gov/default.aspx

The Internet is a fabulous place, which can enrich your life and your business in so many amazing ways. Don't be afraid. Be informed and alert. Take all the necessary steps to protect yourself and move forward with confidence.

CHAPTER 5

LEGITIMATE INTERNET GURUS

Danger – Tribal Leaders

You have come a long way. You are now deep into the heart of the Internet Jungle. Hopefully, you are now better informed and wiser; but, don't let your guard down.

You have encountered, or at least become aware of the lions, tigers, and bears, oh my! You know about the sneaky snakes and cannibals; and you have become acquainted with the friendly and not-so-friendly natives.

You are learning to live and thrive in the jungle, but there is one more group, possibly the most dangerous group of all, the Tribal Leaders – AKA the Internet Gurus who profess to have found the secrets of Internet success and the accumulation of wealth – and some of them have.

You may have met some of them already. They seem to be nice, polite, educated, well-spoken, helpful people. You may even have begun developing relationships with some of them. They are very likeable and offer hope to anyone seeking successful ventures on the Internet.

Some of the Internet Gurus that you meet are legitimate and offer quality products. There are experts in the area of writing, publishing and marketing e-books. There are experts in viral marketing techniques, social media marketing, copywriting, SEO (Search Engine Optimization), affiliate marketing, article writing, FBA (Fulfillment by Amazon) and Website building and monetization. The list goes on and on.

They offer seminars, teleseminars, and Webinars (usually free) as an introduction to their money-generating offers. For those who can (and will) pay for their books, online training, and one-on-one coaching, there are opportunities to learn a lot – but they are expensive.

I do not want to imply that there is nothing of value being sold on the Internet at a reasonable price that may help you establish a successful business. There is useful information (including training programs) available; but, there are hundreds, possibly thousands of books, articles, training courses, and various other products that are either bogus, essentially useless, or, even though they sound good, you may end up never using them for a variety of reasons.

Every sales pitch regardless of who is making it is designed to convince you that "this course, product, or software is exactly what you need to be successful!" Unfortunately, 95% to 99% of the time the promise is just a promise to get you to buy.

Claiming to be an expert does not make it so. The majority of these "gurus" are nothing more than intelligent and clever marketing gurus who have found a way to make millions by convincing others that they have the product or system to make dreams come true.

The challenge is figuring out which ones are the REAL experts who are offering something of value; and which ones are just really good sales people. I don't know what the actual ratio of real experts to professed experts is, but my guess is that it could be as low as 1:100

Many of the "experts" are selling products and programs that they have created from information that is readily available all over the Internet – at no charge – if you just know where to look. They packaged it with a catchy name and sell it for a tidy sum.

There are also products that will not do what they promise and are essentially useless (AKA worthless trash☺) and certainly not worth the asking price

The big dark secret that no one tells you is that the only people making the huge six-figure incomes are the people who have built up an enormous following and are selling products (their own and others) at very high prices through FREE webinars, social media promotions, and direct marketing to their ever-expanding e-mail lists.

Some common categories of Internet Marketing offerings (real and bogus) are: Building and Monetizing Websites, Authority Websites, How to Write and Publish e-Books, Blogging, SEO (Search Engine Optimization), Generating Traffic, Building Your List, and How to Use Social Media. There are more, but you get the idea.

There is one big area of interest (niche) that has become a cash cow for many of these "experts." That niche is: Publishing on Kindle.

It took me a long time (and several thousand dollars) to realize that practically everything the "experts" are teaching about e-book self-publishing is available FREE through Amazon's Kindle Direct Publishing (KDP) – and additional help on converting eBooks to hard copy books is available FREE through CreateSpace, under the tab Free Publishing Resources.

The sad thing is that many of these so-called experts have never written a book and probably never will, but they realized that they could have someone collect easily-accessible free material from the Internet, tweak it slightly, package it well in a saleable format (books, DVD's, training courses, videos, etc.), set a reasonable price (usually $17 to $27), develop a high-powered marketing/sales strategy, and make a lot of money.

Those who have the money, hire talented copy writers to carefully craft sales pages that will convince you that you may actually have a chance at hitting it big – their product may be the one that finally works for you.

They use emotional triggers to exploit you. They prey on your intense desire to succeed and to make "loads of money" Online. They know how to use "squeeze pages" to squeeze every possible penny from your bank account. The most successful of the Internet Gurus have become very adept at psychological warfare.

They do not care whether their systems work or not – whether you are successful or not. Their only goal is to take your money to fill their own pockets.

In your search for the best information available, that is the right fit for your area of interest, keep the following uppermost in your mind:

Anyone with a computer and an Internet connection can advertise instructional programs and sell them to unsuspecting, hardworking newbies who haven't learned the ropes yet.

Before you pay a single penny for anything, be a detective first and find out what is available for FREE. Study it carefully and implement what you learn. If you still need help, then you can begin looking for other materials that can take you further along your chosen path.

Free Webinars Can Be Your Financial Downfall

A common strategy for presenting their product to the world is offering a FREE Webinar, which I have mentioned several times already. These are designed to generate impulse buying. They give you just enough information to convince you that you need more . . . in fact, you need the entire package they are offering at a greatly discounted price available only through the webinar. The intent is to seduce you into buying before you leave the Webinar – before you have time to think about it.

It is a little like going fishing with a shotgun as the attendees at the Webinar who are caught up in the hype and excitement of learning a few new things quickly sign up for the "magic bullet" product and pay anywhere from $97 to $997. If you can believe the gurus, there are as many as 1,000+ people who attend these seminars.

Do the math. If only 10% buy at the lowest price – that is 100 sales at $97 = $9,700. Not bad for a 60-minute presentation. And, they almost always provide a "recorded session" for anyone who happened to miss the live session, from which they glean a few thousand dollars more.

This strategy is particularly effective if the product developers can get someone (or several someone's) who are already established as a guru, to sponsor (and introduce) them or just send out emails to their substantial list announcing the webinar – for a percentage of the "take." I have fallen prey to this marketing tactic more than once.

I am sure you have heard the saying, "Politics makes strange bedfellows." I would amend that slightly and say, "The Internet makes for even stranger bedfellows!" You will see joint venture agreements between fierce competitors who sell the same products to the same market.

It happens frequently when such an agreement financially benefits both parties and together they are more powerful than they are working separately. Joint venture agreements between competitors are not all that uncommon. The problem is that together they are a more formidable threat to newbies because it muddies the line between value-added products being offered by experts and junk being offered by experts in name only.

Never Buy Without a Money-Back Guarantee

The majority of offers made through free webinars provide a 30-day money-back guarantee – some even give a 60- or 90-day guarantee. (Be sure to take a screen shot of their guarantee, just in case you decide to buy.)

Guarantees are a good thing and most are honored – but not always. They can refuse your refund request and say that there was a disclaimer that you missed, which will make it difficult, if not impossible to get your money back – even if what you received was a pile of junk or information that you already had. I lost a $1,000 because of this scenario – so I know it happens.

Be smart! Don't fall for the "Bonus Trap." As more of an incentive to BUY NOW, they will give you several bonus products. Unfortunately, most of the bonuses they promise you fall into one of the following categories:

1. The product(s) are recycled products they have sold in other webinars.
2. They are packages made up of information that is free on the Internet.
3. They are products you do not need because they have nothing to do with your goals and chances are very good that you will never use them.
4. They are totally useless.
5. You may never receive them. (I have several bonuses of "one-on-one coaching that I never received.)

Ignore the URGENCY message: "BUY NOW or Lose the Opportunity."

Ignore the time limit they put on the offer (and there is always a time limit) – but, I guarantee that it will be available for at least a day or two following the webinar.

Do not get sucked into that vortex and spend money without doing the following:

- Checking out the product and the people selling it.

- Seriously thinking about your goals and deciding if this product is something that will move you forward in reaching those goals – and whether or not you will actually have time to use it.

You can be sure the offer will be available tomorrow!

At the very least, take the time to run the presenter(s) name through Google. This will not tell you everything you need to know, but it is a place to start.

Ask other marketers or even your friends on Facebook, Google+, or any other social media platforms you use. Find out if anyone knows these experts or gurus – and if they have taken a course or purchased a product from them. Do some digging and get as much information as possible.

NEVER, NEVER, EVER impulse buy!

Never, never, ever buy anything that does not have a money-back guarantee.

If you decide to purchase after waiting at least a day and checking everything out – and *if you really believe the product will help you reach your specific goals – and you will have time to use it,* take the following steps.

- Put the screen shot of the guarantee and a copy of your invoice in a file where you can find them quickly. Also be sure to keep all the contact information (name, physical address, phone number, and email address) of the company or individual who sold you the product.

- Mark your calendar with a reminder of when the guarantee period is over, so you can request a refund within the allotted time, if you choose.

- Carve out an adequate amount of time to use the materials immediately so you can make an informed decision about whether there is enough value for you to keep the products – given your specific goals.

- *If you don't have time to try the product – don't buy it no matter how good it seems to be.*

WORD of WARNING: They are counting on the fact that most people will not be able to fully test their system within the 30 days they allow for refunds. They also know that most people will miss the refund deadline or be too embarrassed to request a refund. DO NOT let any of those things happen to you.

Chapter 6
The Shiny Object Syndrome

Strategic Business Decision or Costly Distraction

One of the most important lessons to be learned is how to identify a real business opportunity and how to recognize offers that are nothing more than distractions that can pull you off course and result in the loss of time and money.

As you get more and more involved in your business, regardless of your area of focus – Social Media Marketing, E-commerce, Writing, Publishing, Virtual Assistant, Website Design, Affiliate Marketing, etc. – you will be bombarded with offers that promise to "help you be successful." This was discussed in a previous section, but it is important to look at it again from a little different perspective because those offerings are dangerous and enticing traps.

Do not allow yourself to be distracted.

DO NOT "buy-in" to every offer that comes along just because it sounds good and you HOPE that the new offer will solve all your problems!

Keep your long-term goal(s) in mind at all times. Goals should always be considered in the purchase of books, training programs, software, or other materials. If they do not tie-in directly with the accomplishment of your goals and the strategy that you are currently using . . . do not make the purchase. It will only be a distraction and take you off course.

REMEMBER – the offer (or one very similar) will always be available if you decide you want to explore it in the future.

The Shiny Object Syndrome as described by Adam Short of *Niche Profit Classroom* is possibly the most common distraction for people who are new to the Internet Business Jungle.

The following is an excerpt from one of his recent blog posts:

"The Shiny Object Syndrome symbolizes loss of focus and attention, and an attraction to every shiny, new strategy that comes along.

This attraction takes your attention away from following through with the strategies on which you are working.

Here is an example of the syndrome at work...

Let's say you have two websites and you are working on linking strategies but you are getting frustrated waiting for your Google rankings to rise. In your email inbox comes another shiny, new strategy for you to try that promises to help you increase traffic. Due to your current frustration, you drop what you are doing with the linking and decide to give this new strategy a try. You are hoping this new "thing" will be a quick fix to your problem.

Unfortunately, this vicious cycle continues until one day you realize you have started tons of new strategies with no earnings to speak of. The problem is not the strategies; it is the lack of follow through required to make them work.

It's important to note here that new strategies are always good to consider and they aren't necessarily toxic to your current strategies. These "new" techniques are only detrimental if they cause you to abandon the strategies in progress in hopes of something "better".

The solution to this problem, or maybe I should say the preventative action to help you avoid developing the "shiny object syndrome" is two-fold:

1. **Learn as much as you can about your area of interest when you are first enter the Internet arena.** <u>Start with the free information available on the Internet.</u> After you have thoroughly digested the FREE information - then, and only then, should you consider purchasing any products or training.

2. When you are ready, **choose one strategy and stay with it long enough to see results (a minimum of six months – preferably a year.)**

Learn to Recognize REAL Opportunities that Are Strategically Sound

It is easy to become so hyper-aware of dangers in the Internet Jungle that you fail to recognize strategically sound opportunities when they show up.

Keep in mind that **all of the natives are not** UNFRIENDLY; some of the lions, tigers, bears, and snakes can be helpful creatures. Plus, some of the Tribal Leaders are genuine experts.

Danger and opportunity live side-by-side in the Internet Business Jungle. The key to success is developing the ability to recognize the difference between the two. You must be able to avoid the traps and being eaten alive; but you also want to be able to recognize the viable opportunities that fit with your goals.

Use the following questions to help you recognize strategically sound opportunities and to avoid costly distractions:

To summarize – before you buy anything *review the following checklist.*

→ **Can I find this information on the Internet and pay nothing?**

→ **How can this information (product) help me?**

Is it directly connected to my area of focus (e.g. Writing and Publishing, Selling Products on Amazon, Building and Monetizing Websites, Blogging, etc.)

This is a tough one because in the beginning you don't know what you need. My advice is to *choose an area that really interests you. Use that as your focal point and stick with it for at least 6 months – refuse to buy anything that is not directly related to that area.*

→ *Do I have time to study and use the product (information, training)?*

Given everything else you have going on with your current strategy, is it realistic for you to take on something new at this point in time? The same offering (or something similar) will be available at a later date – so, be willing to wait if time is an issue.

→ *Do not develop the Shiny Object Syndrome*

DO NOT jump from one strategy to another thinking that "this one" will be better than what you are currently using - hoping to find the magic bullet.

If you know you have a problem with "shiny objects" simply DO NOT LOOK at anything new until you have completely exhausted the tools and strategies you are currently using. Remove yourself from every mailing list and if anything new shows up – delete it immediately.

→ **Is there at least a 30-day money back guarantee?**

Never buy anything that does not have at least a 30-day money back guarantee.

Warning, even if there is a guarantee, it will not always be honored. Most of the time it will be honored, but occasionally it will not be.

→ **Does the information/course/product have the potential to do what it is supposed to do?**

This is where the guarantee comes in. You cannot always answer this question until you get into the meat of a product. Mark the final return date on your calendar and then, check out the materials immediately. Don't wait! Go through as much of the material as you can as quickly as possible. If it isn't directly related to your area of focus; if it doesn't live up to the promises; or, if you can't use it for any reason (no time, not ready for it, etc.) – ask for a refund!

→ **Will I be required to spend additional money to implement the information?**

There is always an upsell. Once you pay and are given notice to download your product, there will always be one, two or three additional products that you "should buy to get the most out of the original product that you purchased." Don't buy additional products. Either skip past them all and just take the original product; or, if it seems at all schlocky to you, ask for a refund immediately.

→ **Does the 'course' assume that I have more computer skills, experience, or basic knowledge than I actually possess?** (This one is IMPORTANT)

Is the course beyond where you are on the learning curve for the area you have decided to pursue? This can and will happen. If it seems like something   is over your head, then get a refund. You can always buy the product or something very similar when you are ready.

→ **Is the person offering (or teaching) the course really knowledgeable or well-known?**

(Check them out) How long have they been around, what is their reputation, have they really made money using the system they are trying to sell; or is it hype to make money by selling you (and others) a product?

→ *Ignore the hard sell!*

There will most likely be a "hard sell" to get you to sign up today. Even though they will lead you to believe that you must buy NOW or miss the opportunity, they always give you two or three days to make the purchase. Take the time to check out the person, the company, and the product! In my opinion, the hard sell is a red flag and you should run in the other direction.

→ *After your investigation, what does your gut tell you?*

Is the company or the person selling the product credible? Do you really believe that s/he has personally used the product, system, software to make money, or is it something they have put together to "make money."

→ **Does the promotion sound too good to be true?**

If they are promising you a quick six-figure return on your investment in a matter of months, or anything else that is not quite believable, you know the saying, "If it sounds too good to be true, it probably is." In this case – there is no probably about it! It is too good to be true.

Take Inventory and Track Your Purchases

Depending on how long you have been trekking through the Internet Jungle, the number of products you have purchased from "Internet Experts" will vary. But, whatever the number, it is very likely that most of them are doing very little except weighing down your hard drive. My guess is that you probably have yet to make a single penny from any of them.

The majority of newbies have no idea how much they are spending – big mistake! My recommendation is that you immediately take inventory of all your purchases to date - using an Excel Spreadsheet which includes the following columns of information:

- **Date Purchased**

- **Category of Use** (Marketing; Training; Domains; Book Covers; etc.)

- **Product Name and Type** (Software; Training Program; e-book; One-on-one coaching; etc.)

- **Company** (Presenter)/Author

- **Sold Through** (Free or paid webinar/e-mail solicitation/recommendation from….)

- **Guarantee** (30-, 60-, or 90-day guarantee and final date for return)

- **Website of Purchase** (Follow-up contact info)

- **Value Added** (Used it; Read it; Implemented it; or No Value)

- **Comments** (Helped me; Made money from it; Saved me time; Other benefits – or No Benefits)

- **Amount Paid** (With TOTAL – at the bottom)

- **Refund** (With TOTAL – at the bottom)

- **Action Taken** (Cancelled' SCAM reported; etc.)

Once you have finished your inventory, continue to track purchases. It is best if you enter the information on a weekly or monthly basis so that you have an up-to-date running total. You need a clear picture of the amount of money you are spending each and every month and the return on your investment (ROI).

If you do not do this, I promise you will spend far more than you realize and far more than you should – plus the benefits will be minimal.

Conclusion – Part One

There are opportunities to create and build a successful online business. I want to commend you for your willingness to put yourself out there and for having the guts to follow your dream.

Wanting a better life for you and your family is a good thing. I encourage you to continue searching until you find a viable, legitimate business, if you have not already found one.

However, never lose sight of the fact that Internet commerce is like any business arena – you must pay your dues. Success will not come overnight, or over many nights. It will take focus, commitment, and patience that are supported by a substantial investment of money, time, energy, and lots of hard work.

There are many, very smart people in the Internet Jungle that will try to convince you otherwise. Remember they are lying. Their only concern is "What's in it for them." There are no shortcuts to success.

PART TWO

CHAPTER 7

LET THE ADVENTURE BEGIN!

Educate Yourself – Study, Listen, Learn

There is a good chance that you have been told all your life, "Get an education." That is sound advice, but what they fail to mention is that every day you live is part of your education. Experience is one of the great teachers in life and is critical in this new business environment.

There are always others out there who have information you do not have, or who know things you do not know. Those with experience have learned what TO DO and what NOT TO DO.... things you have yet to learn.

A formal education – college degree, advanced degree, or specialized training can be helpful; but, when you decide to start an online business, be prepared for the very steep learning curve you will face. You must be willing to educate yourself about how business is done in this new frontier.

To be successful, you need to set aside a specific amount of time every day to study – to learn something you need to know – something that will help you reach your goal. It may be about marketing on the Internet, using social media, how to set up a Website, how to write and self-publish e-books, or developing expertise in your selected niche.

The list is endless and I promise you that the more you know, the more you will realize how much you don't know! You must NEVER lose your interest in learning and the pursuit of knowledge.

Knowledge is power! Knowledge is what makes surviving and thriving in the Internet Jungle possible.

Plan Your Adventure

There is an anonymous quote that is frequently used. "Those who fail to plan, plan to fail." I agree it is trite; but, it is also true. A business plan is vital to success. It should be your road map that you reference often. It will keep you on course, and ultimately take you where you want to go.

When developing a map, you must first determine where you are right now and be as clear as possible about where you want to end up. Take the time to identify your assets and liabilities; your strengths and weaknesses; what you know and what do you need to know – and then, plan the route (action steps) that will take you to your destination.

If you don't know where you are going, how will you know when you get there? Your destination is your long-range goal. Make it as clear as possible and write it down. If you can't see beyond the next six months – then set your goals for where you want to be (or think you want to be) in six months and begin writing your plan.

The next step is to identify the action steps that will take you from Point A to Point B to Point C, and so on, until you reach that six-month goal. The journey cannot be made in one giant leap. It must be accomplished a step-at-a-time. Each of those action steps must be written down as well. If you do not know what the first step is, it may be easier to work backward from the final goal. Use whatever method works for you – but write your plan! When you are nearing the end of the six-month journey, develop your plan for the next six months, one year, or three years (as far out as you can see clearly).

Most entrepreneurs do not fully understand the path and direction of their new business. Don't let that become an excuse for not writing a plan.

Writing a business plan is one of the best ways I know to develop a plan of action. Use it as a tool to start brainstorming and becoming more creative in your approach to the business you want to build.

You should always remember that a business plan is not a hard line in the sand. It is a moving line and should continually be adjusted and improved.

Find a Guide

Having a road map (business plan) is great; and it is also incredibly helpful to find a guide. Having the combination of a road map AND a guide will almost guarantee that you will arrive at your destination without taking a lot of detours and side trips.

A jungle guide (or mentor) can be your strongest asset. If you can clearly define where you are and where you want to be, a mentor will be able to show you the most direct path to get there.

Well-seasoned and well-established Internet marketers, gurus, and experts have information and training materials that can guide you in making good business decisions ("that will lead" or "to") lead you down the right path.

It would be wise to actively look for such a guide. Explore the options, ask lots of questions, and talk to others who have worked with some of the experts you are considering. Avoid impulse buying and choosing randomly – just because it sounds good.

Once you have made your decision about a particular program – stay with it.

Many *years* ago I gave my daughters a framed needlepoint that read, "Choose your love. Love your choice!"

That statement can also be applied in this setting. Once your choice is made and you have made that initial investment, embrace it and stay with it – ***for at least a year***.

Follow the expert's lead. Work through the training step-by-step. Diligently apply what you learn. Find out what works for you and what doesn't.

Do not get distracted; do not jump ship and grab each "shiny object" that comes along. Many of the available programs work; but only if you stay with them, study hard, and keep your eyes on the prize (stay focused).

You can do it and be successful if you are disciplined, stay consistent, and remain ever vigilant.

Good luck and enjoy the ride!

Nancy

P. S. Be sure to pick up the next book in the series:

Congratulations! You Are Self-Employed

Part Two - Starting an Online Business

ABOUT THE AUTHOR

Nancy N. Wilson

All things beautiful are my passion. I enjoy anything that a masterful hand creates - writing, photography, visual arts, cooking, the human body, the human spirit, technology, our beautiful world . . . and so much more.

As a young child, I was very curious and always wanted to know why something worked and how it worked. My mother encouraged me to explore almost anything that interested me - she allowed me to take apart old clocks and radios so that I could figure out how they worked.

She also gave me free reign in the kitchen to create my masterpieces of flour, sugar, spices, and anything else I could find in the cupboards. The more I learned, the more I wanted to know, which led me quickly to the discovery of the wealth of information available in books, plus the magical journeys I could take through the power of words!

Reading became the center of my life. The town library was located in the Women's Club of the little farming community that I called home. In my eyes, it was the grandest building in town - newly built, with a heavenly air-conditioner that sheltered me from the blazing heat of Arizona summers. It was my personal cocoon in which I could read the hours away.

My first adventure in writing came my senior year in high school when I decided to take a writing correspondence course, which was very forward-looking for the time. I experienced the first thrill of putting pen to paper. It was a magical new adventure! My love affair with the written word began.

Unfortunately, my affair was dealt a serious blow during my first year in college when an English professor told me that I used a lot of words, but said very little. His words went to my very core and hobbled my writing confidence for a number of years. I continued to write, but not with the same excitement and enthusiasm that I had previously enjoyed.

It was not until many years later that everything turned around. After completing my MBA as a "mature woman" I found a position with a Leadership Development Training Company in Manhattan that required use of three of my major passions: my insatiable curiosity of how and why things work, my love of learning through books, and my need to write and be published.

I know, my work was not published in the true sense of the word, but my words were in print and people were reading them and using them to improve their professional lives. I had finally begun to realize my dream.

Now I am retired and living the dream on a daily basis. I write many hours every day. All my work is non-fiction. Even though I love fiction, that has never been my focus and there are others who do it so much better than I. My choice has always been, and will continue to be, to write about topics that interest and intrigue me and to share what I discover with my readers.

OTHER BOOKS BY THIS AUTHOR

Cookbooks
Candy Making Made Easy - Instructions and 17 Starter Recipes
Cake Making Made Easy - Instructions and 60 Cakes
Cook Ahead – Freezer to Table
The Healthy Diet Cookbook
Garden Fresh Soups and Stews

Mama's Legacy Series
Seven Volumes Available
Dinner – 55 Easy Recipes (Volume I)
Breakfast and Brunch – 60 Delicious Recipes (Volume II)
Dessert – 50 Scrumptious Choices (Volume III)
Chicken – 25 Classic Dinners (Volume IV)
Mexican Favorites – 21 Traditional Recipes (Volume V)
Side Dish Recipes (Volume VI)
Sauce Recipes – 50 Tasty Choices (Volume VII)

Health and Fitness
DETOX – The Master Cleanse Diet
The Secret to Successful Dieting
Juicing for Life

Business
Attitude Adjustment
A Guide to the Kinstant Formatter
Congratulations! You Are Self-Employed

Books Written Under Pen Names
Everything You Need to Know About Growing Roses
Power Up Your Brain - Five Simple Strategies

www.ingramcontent.com/pod-product-compliance
Lightning Source LLC
Chambersburg PA
CBHW070251190526
45169CB00001B/370